READING BETWEEN THE LINES

An Introduction to Bar Code Technology

BY CRAIG K. HARMON
and
RUSS ADAMS

HELMERS PUBLISHING, INC.

(formerly North American Technology, Inc.)
174 Concord St., Peterborough, NH 03458

Bar code on cover courtesy of Symbology, Inc., St. Paul, MN

TABLE OF CONTENTS

SECTION VII—Applications

APPENDIXES

FOREWORD

In 1949 N.J. Woodland, et al. filed a patent for a circular bar code. In the 35 years that have followed, we have witnessed "bars and spaces" popping up everywhere. Over 50 unique symbologies have been developed, and to face this new "Tower of Babel" various industry groups have begun a process of standardization to one or two of the choices available. The grocery and retail industries have established the Uniform Code Council (UCC), the automotive industry Automotive Industry Action Group (AIAG), and the health industry the Health Industry Bar Code (HIBC) Council. Government has standardized with the LOGMARS Report, and NATO countries appear to be following the U.S. Department of Defense lead. Standards have been developed for the French pharmaceutical manufacturers. Industry groups have wrestled with the establishment of nationwide and worldwide standards through the efforts of the Distribution Symbology Study Group and the American National Standards Institute. And finally, a focal point for the distribution of information on bar coding has been established by the Automatic Identification Manufacturers.

Since 1980 there has been a torrent of information on bar coding. This book is an attempt to organize that information. It will introduce you to bar code and its benefits. We express our appreciation to the Automatic Identification Manufacturers (AIM) for their help in developing this text. Thanks also go to Dr. David Allais, President of Intermec, for his assistance.

In this updated, third edition, we have added new information and removed names and addresses of groups that no longer exist. Of major import is the addition of two new appendices—Appendix E, which addresses solutions to the problem of skew, and Appendix F, which includes the specifications for Code 39. A new chapter, Chapter 18, is concerned with justifying and implementing a bar code system.

The reader should note that the superscripts throughout Section I of this book refer to the footnotes listed in Appendix G.

If this book helps you understand bar code and the advantages it offers, then we have accomplished our task.

Craig K. Harmon
Russ Adams

SECTION I

OVERVIEW

SECTION II

OVERVIEW

CHAPTER 1

INTRODUCTION

Without fanfare, bar codes have become an important part of our lives. They have crept into businesses as diverse as automobile factories and corner grocery stores. Bar code is the unsung hero of many computer-based business systems. Bar codes and automatic identification systems are the most cost-effective management tools for the 1980s. Their use is quickly rewarded by improved asset management and resource allocation. In an age of steadily declining productivity, companies that have adopted bar code–based management systems have quickly seen a reversal of this trend.

A bar code is a self-contained message with information encoded in the widths of bars and spaces in a printed pattern. Since bar codes are used with computers, binary code is used. Essentially, the black bars and white spaces represent ones and zeros—the language computers understand.

In their simplest form, bar codes are read by sweeping a small spot of light across the printed bar code symbol. The sweep starts at the white space before the first bar, continues past the last bar and ends in the white space which follows the last bar. Because a bar code cannot be read if the sweep wanders outside the symbol area, bar heights are chosen to make it easy to keep the sweep within the bar code area. The longer the information to be coded, the longer the bar code. As the length increases, the height of the bars must be increased to allow for more wandering during reading.

There are many different ways to arrange black bars and white spaces to code information. Each method of arranging bar code patterns has properties which achieve specific objectives. The many bar code formats used today attempt to:

1. Read only if the entire symbol is scanned.
2. Be scannable in both directions.
3. Clearly define the difference between bars and spaces.
4. Be readable over a wide range of scanning speeds.

The most familiar bar code format is the Universal Product Code, or UPC. This code is used widely in retail food and general merchandise stores. A quick look at cereal boxes, record album jackets, and magazine covers will acquaint you with bar code symbols in the UPC format.

In many supermarket checkout lanes, store clerks pass each grocery item over a laser scanner which reads the UPC bar code on the item's packaging. Let's say the item is a box of Cheerios. When the box is passed over the scanner, the digits 16000 66510 are read from the UPC symbol on the box. The first five digits indicate that the manufacturer is General Mills, and the second five digits indicate the product and volume of the package. The product number is transmitted to the store's computer. The price and name are looked up in the computer's memory and transmitted back to the correct cash register. The electronic cash register prints the name and price at the time on the register tape. If Cheerios is on sale, the cash register rings up the sale price. In addition, the computer automatically deducts one box of Cheerios from the store's inventory. The store's computer may be connected to the wholesaler's computer and automatically place an order when inventory drops below a predetermined level.

Such a bar code system increases productivity in three ways:

Speed: Data is entered into the computer more rapidly.

Accuracy: Bar code systems are almost error-free. They do not rely on the accuracy of a human entering data on a keyboard.

Reliability: Bar code formats are designed with various forms of error checking built into the code.

There are forms other than bar code for automatic identification, but bar code was designed to be read by simply constructed readers. The only hardware required to read bar code is a source of light and a single photoreceptor. Almost everything else can be done by software. It is the low-cost, simple nature of bar code–based systems, along with the productivity benefits they offer, which has brought about the "bar code explosion" we see around us. This book will introduce you to the technology that makes bar code identification work and show you how bar code is being used to save money by increasing productivity.

CHAPTER 2

A HISTORY OF BAR CODE

The UPC patch found on almost every product symbolizes the major advancements made in the automation of product distribution over the past two decades. The vast variety of products available in today's supermarket is the result of automated systems in production, packaging, and handling. But these innovations did not occur overnight. They were the result of the steady application of automation techniques throughout the food retailing industry.

The modern supermarket began with the concept of the self-service food store. In 1916, this concept was introduced by Clarence Sanders in his Piggly Wiggly stores. By the 1930s, the trend to the self-service supermarket was well under way with individually priced items and mechanized checkout counters. From 1934 to 1974, these improvements reduced the cost of distribution from 24 percent to 20.9 percent of gross sales.

In 1932, an ambitious project was begun by a small group of students at the Harvard University Graduate School of Business Administration. It was to foreshadow the automated checkout counter. The project proposed that the customer select the desired merchandise from an order catalog. Punch cards indicating the desired merchandise were to be removed by the customer and handed to the checker. The punch cards were placed into a punch card reader which entered the codes for the selected merchandise into the system. The system then provided belt delivery of the merchandise from a storeroom to the checkout counter. A complete customer bill was produced and inventory records were generated.

The students offered the plan to food chains around the country, but the plan was rejected by them all. Labor in 1930 was only 30 or 40 cents an hour. With such cheap labor costs, the capital investment to implement the students' system was not justified. The idea did not die, however. As labor costs advanced, the potential savings in the use of an automated checkout counter made the idea attractive. Manual price marking, manual cash register tallying, manual inventory control, and fuzzy information about store operations challenged innovative minds in the food store industry to develop better systems. In the late 1940s, the National Association of Food Chains (NAFC) began to study inventions which could improve the speed and reduce the cost of food checkout.

One invention examined by the Association was a system which used metal tags attached to every product in the supermarket. The price of each product was indicated by the tag's thickness. The merchandise was placed in a mesh bag, the bag was placed in a cabinet at the checkout counter, and an electric current sensed the total thickness of all of the tags in the bag. The sensed thickness value was used to calculate the total bill for the merchandise. However, the cost of the tags and attaching them to the merchandise in the store exceeded the total cost of the manual checkout system. And a customer who purchased products packed in metal cans ended up with an inflated bill.

By the 1950s the transistor had been invented and electronics was making explosive progress. It was time to look again at the possibility of automating food store checkout. In 1955, at the annual meeting of the U. S. Chamber of Commerce, a program titled "People, Products and Progress—1975" was presented. It offered predictions about what the world would be like in 20 years. The section of the program about food distribution featured an automated checkout stand with an overhead electronic scanner attached to a cash register. "When the shopping is over," the commentator said, "there will be no lengthy waiting at the checkout counter. The improvement here will be an automatic computer that will price all items as they pass under an electronic eye." Quite prophetic.

In the mid 1960s, the electronic checkout was still an idea for the future, but it was an idea that was beginning to look like it would save money and improve productivity. The Safeway chain, for example, had 400,000 checkout counters, over $60 billion per year in sales, over 450 million staff hours, and a payroll that exceeded $1 billion. At the 1966 NAFC Management Clinic on Physical Research, equipment manufacturers were asked to aid in the development of systems to improve supermarket operating efficiency. John L. Strubbe, vice president of The Kroger Company, characterized the benefits of automated systems in this way:

> Our stores are really the conduits for concentrated, high volume operations involving essentially repetitive processing movements. They represent the classic environment for success of production equipment and electronic controls. Store labor is expensive and scarce...I am not overstating the case when I say that the security of our employees depends upon our ability to increase our productivity, with the help of mechanical and electronic equipment and systems which do not exist today.

In the late 1960s, a number of companies and individuals began to seriously develop practical automated supermarket systems. Generally, the electronics equipment manufacturer worked with a food chain and kept the development work secret. In 1967, a pilot system was installed in a Kroger store in Cincinnati.

But all the systems under development had some common problems to solve. The entire food industry had to agree on a uniform coding system for product identification. It had to be accurately read by a variety of scanning systems. It had to be readable from any direction. And it had to be printable on a wide variety of package sizes and paper stocks. Even more important, the coding system had to be available free to all who needed to use it. The advantages and disadvantages to the consumer, distributor, and manufacturer of each proposed system had to be evaluated objectively. These common problems could only be solved by establishing a group representing all segments of the food industry. This group would have to set policy, keep records, and approve basic rules.

In 1969, the Board of Directors of the NAFC contracted with Logicon, Inc. to develop a proposal for a universal coding system. This resulted in Parts 1 and 2 of the "Universal Grocery Products Identification Code" (UGPIC) in the summer of 1970. The proposal served as an outline for the dimensions of such an automated coding system and provided specific recommendations. The proposal challenged the food industry and got action.

Based on the recommendations of the Logicon report, the U. S. Supermarket Ad Hoc Committee on Universal Product Coding was formed. Three years later, the Committee recommended the adoption of the UPC symbol set. By June 1974, one of the first scanners capable of reading the Universal Product Code was installed at Marsh's supermarket in Troy, Ohio. The scanning system was added to the store's existing computer-driven cash register. By 1980 it was estimated that better than 90 percent of all grocery items carried a UPC code. By December 1985, according to *SCAN Newsletter,* more than 12,000 grocery stores were equipped with scanner checkout systems.

While the American food industry was developing its bar code–based automatic product identification system, another industry was experimenting with a different automatic identification system. The North American railroad industry began to study the concept of automatic car identification in the late 1950s. By 1962, the Association of American Railroads formed a department to study and develop standards for such a system. The Association adopted an optical bar code system in 1967. The decision was surrounded by controversy from the beginning. The original specification had stipulated that no maintenance would be required for the vehicle label. As the car identification project progressed and optical systems were considered, this requirement was modified. It was evident to the project participants that label maintenance, including washing, would be required.

Car labeling and scanner installation began on October 10, 1967. The task was immense. Labels had to be applied to more than two million freight cars scattered over millions of miles of railroad. As a result, it took seven years before 95 percent of the fleet was labeled. While the labeling continued, railroads around the country began to develop improved management information systems. The systems were designed to improve how well the freight cars were used and to help raise the level of service provided to customers.

These management information systems relied on accurate data about car location. Since 70 percent of rail shipments used tracks owned by two or more companies, success depended on industry-wide labeling and proper label maintenance. Since so many railroad operating companies were involved, it was difficult for any prediction to be made about how well the proposed automatic car identification system would perform.

Because no prediction could be made, many railroad operation companies took a wait-and-see attitude. They did not install all of the scanners called for in the original plan. Since few railroads were using scanners, labels were not maintained as called for in the original plan. By 1975, 20 percent of the labels were unreadable. Several studies were undertaken to determine how to solve the problems and make the system work. Many of the findings were controversial. The most controversial finding suggested that some operating companies did not want the system to succeed because of railroad tariff rules. The end result was the virtual abandonment of bar code for freight car identification.

SECTION II

THE WORLD OF
BAR CODES

CHAPTER 3

SYMBOLOGY

Symbology is defined as the art of expression by symbols or the study or interpretations of symbols. A symbol is defined as something that stands for or suggests something else by reason of relationship, association, or convention. A bar code symbol is an array of rectangular bars and spaces that are arranged in a specific way to represent elements of data. A bar code character represents, for example, a letter, a number, or some other graphic symbol in a machine-readable form.

But what advantage is there to a symbol which can be read by a machine? And why can't machines read the same letters, numbers, and graphic symbols that humans read? Machine-readable symbols help input information more quickly. Information so collected is more accurate and costs less than if manually entered using keys. For many years computers have automated the number crunching tasks associated with business management. Data collection, however, has been quite a different matter. The data "crunched" by computers have continued to be entered manually. Traditionally, data are collected by writing them down on paper. The paper is given to a supervisor who checks their accuracy. If the paper is readable, it's given to a key-entry operator who types the information into a computer. Managers then use the entered data to make decisions. How much time has elapsed? What is the reliability of the information that finally was entered? How much did it cost to get that information to managers?

Under the best conditions, a minimum of three days is required between collection of the information until the data are in a form usable by management. Often the time is closer to two or three weeks. These delays are bound to affect the accuracy of decisions made by management.

Traditional manual data collection lacks high reliability. Translation errors occur when the information is written down and when it is key entered. The number of translation errors is directly proportional to the number of characters written down during data collection. The longer the string of characters, the higher the probability that it contains an error when it is written down. When a key-entry operator reads the transcribed data, often the operator must interpret what was written. Is that an S or a 5, an O or a 0, a B or an 8, an H or a K, an F or a T? Transposition errors can also occur, such as recording 1234 as 1243. But translation and transposition errors are not the only errors inherent in manual data collection. Additional errors are introduced in the key-entry process. It is common for a key-entry operator to make one character error in every 300 characters entered.

In analyzing the benefits of automatic data entry, you must consider the personnel cost to write the information down, check the forms, and key enter the information into the computer system. There are the costs of the errors and the costs of correcting the errors. Finally, there are very substantial costs associated with management not having current information when decisions are made.

Machine-read information can be sent to the computer as the data is captured. The reliability of the data is at least 50 times better and can be more than a billion times better than manual systems. Costs are reduced so much that frequently machine-readable systems produce a positive change in a firm's cash flow within a matter of months. Industry is accustomed to amortizing equipment over several years before realizing a payback. It's no wonder there is a rush to install machine-readable systems.

Why can't machines read the same letters, numbers, and graphic symbols that humans read? Of course, they can. But with what reliability and with what speed of entry? There are numerous vision systems available that have the capability of recognizing human-readable characters. One such system is the OCR reader. OCR stands for optical character recognition. OCR uses special fonts that can be read by both human and machine. OCR is a more reliable method of data entry than the key-entry process, but it is invariably less reliable than bar code. Someone using an OCR reader frequently has to make multiple passes over the human-readable information to read it. The reading difficulty of OCR is the result of the technology employed in OCR. The OCR reader must be within a very precise orientation to the symbol being read, much more precise than that required by bar code. Most OCR characters in use today are between 0.10 inch and 0.15 inch in height. When long strings of information are read, it is difficult to maintain correct placement of the wand over the entire string. OCR is far more sensitive to the motion of the operator's hand during scanning than bar code. Finally, vision systems cannot easily read information printed on moving objects. To do so requires, for example, a strobe light synchronized with the object's movement. While OCR is significantly better than key entry, bar code is better in data integrity and speed of data acquisition. Table 3-1 shows comparisons between key entry, OCR, and bar coding.

Table 3-1
Data entry comparisons

Characteristic/ Method	Key-entry	OCR	Bar Code
Speed*	6 seconds	4 seconds	.3 seconds to 2 seconds
Substitution error rate	1 character error in 300 characters entered	1 character error in 10,000 characters entered	1 character error in 15,000 to 36 trillion characters entered
Size*	1 inch to 1.2 inches	1 inch to 1.2 inches	.7 inch to[†] 7 inches
Encoding costs	High	Moderate	Low
Reading costs	Low	Moderate	Low
Advantages	Human	Human-readable	Low error rate Low cost High speed Can be read at a distance
Disadvantages	Human High cost High error rate Low speed	Low speed Moderate error rate Cannot read moving objects without special equipment	Requires Education of the User Community

*Note—Comparisons for speed and size assume the encodation of a 12-character field.
[†]Note—The lower limit of size is a function of the symbology specification. Future scanning systems may permit 12 characters to be encoded in 0.2 inch.

One of the basic advantages of bar code over OCR is that bar code reads information by measurement of width. Further, the bar width is repeated vertically (vertical redundancy). Vertical redundancy permits the bar/space pattern to be read with less precise orientation of the reader as well as providing improved tolerance for localized printing defects. Unlike OCR, bar codes also have a repeating pattern that exists in every character, e.g., Code 39 has nine elements and three are wide and Interleaved 2 of 5 has five elements and 2 are wide. OCR must be read by identifying features of the characters. OCR must identify the horizontal and vertical strokes, curves, and endings of the characters. Bar code systems often use a progression of checking characteristics to improve the reliability of reading. Bar codes can be checked at both the character level and the message level, in much the same way that data communication systems check reliability, by examining each character to establish the presence of a certain pattern of bars and spaces, wide elements and narrow elements, or a defined parity pattern. Message level checking systems add a character or combination of characters at the end of a message. This check character is derived from a mathematical computation based on the characters in the message. Message level checking can be used with key entry, OCR, or bar code systems.

The Structure of Bar Codes

A bar code consists of a number of printed bars and intervening spaces. The widths of the bars and spaces, as well as the number of each, is determined by a specific convention, referred to as a specification for that symbology. The specification sets the minimum nominal width of the narrowest elements (bars and spaces), the ratio of the wide elements to the narrow ones, the printing tolerances (the change in width because of the printing process), the structure of unique bar and space combinations to represent various characters, the bar/space patterns that signify the beginning and the end of the bar code message, and the clear area, or quiet zone, required in front of and at the end of the symbol.

The basic element of a bar code is the width of the narrow element. This width is called the X dimension. Frequently, the widths of the wider elements are measured in multiples of X (see Figure 3-1). In some codes, however, the width of each element is precisely defined. Some symbologies have only two widths, one for the narrow elements and one for the wide elements. Still other symbologies have four widths or more. Beyond simply varying the widths of

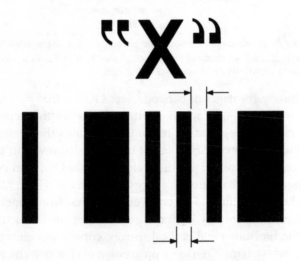

Figure 3-1. Elements of a bar code character

the elements, individual characters can be coded by using differing numbers of bar code elements. Different bar code symbologies use five, seven, eight, and nine elements to code a single character. Some symbologies can represent letters, numbers and other graphic symbols. Most bar code symbologies, however, encode strictly numeric data and a few special characters. Most codes have a unique start/stop character combination, although a few permit multiple start/stop codes with varying purposes.

Bar codes are said to be either discrete or continuous. Simply stated, discrete bar codes start with a bar, end with a bar, and have a space between characters, referred to as an intercharacter gap. By contrast, continuous codes start with a bar, end with a space, and have no intercharacter gap. Bar code symbologies can achieve differing densities (numbers of characters per inch of code). The density of a bar code is determined by the minimum X dimension, the wide-to-narrow element ratio, the number of elements required to represent a character of information, and the overhead characters needed by the symbology, such as start and stop codes and check characters.

There are two measures of a bar code symbology's "friendliness." The first is its "human friendliness," often referred to as its first and second pass read rate. The first pass read rate (FRR) is the ratio of the number of times in which a good read occurs on the first try, divided by the number of attempts. The second pass read rate (SRR) is the ratio of the number of times in which a good scan occurs in two or fewer tries, divided by the number of attempts. Bar code systems should achieve at least an 85 percent FRR and at least a 99 percent SRR. Low read rates ultimately lead to user dissatisfaction and a bar code system which will not be used. While low read rates indicate a high level of no scans, user dissatisfaction is the main concern.

Far more difficult to measure is the symbology's "system friendliness" or substitution error rate (SER). A substitution error exists when the data encoded in the printed symbol does not agree with the data read by the bar code reader. The SER measure is the number of substitution errors which occur over all symbols read. Some bar code symbologies have a proven SER of better than one character in one million scanned. A no scan can be detected by the operator or bar code reading system. But a bad scan, or substitution error, is not detected until after the data has been stored in the data processing system. Even then, the error may not be caught. There is a direct relationship between a symbology's FRR and its SER, since the bar code reading system vigorously attempts to decode the scanned message. Generally stated, the first read rate of a bar code system is a reflection on the printed symbol. Substitution errors, on the other hand, are more attributable to the bar code reader. The more times required to scan a symbol, the higher the probability that a substitution error will occur. However, bar code substitution error rates are much lower than the rate of one substitution error for every 300 characters entered experienced in manual key entry. Even the weakest symbologies are substantially better.

Code 39 (Also known as Code 3 of 9 and 3 of 9 Code)

Code 39 was developed in 1975 by Dr. David Allais and Ray Stevens of Interface Mechanisms (now Intermec). It is rapidly becoming "The Code" for industrial and commercial applications. Code 39 was selected as the official Department of Defense (DoD) symbology in 1981, with the publication of the "Final Report of the Joint Steering Group for Logistics Applications of Automated Marking and Reading Symbols" (acronym LOGMARS). It was established as the official government standard with the issuance of MIL-STD-1189 (now MIL-STD-1189A) in early 1982. Within the federal government, the General Services Administration (GSA) also uses MIL-STD-1189A markings on all material coming into GSA supply depots. The Department of Defense now requires its contractors to mark all items with a Code 39 bar code, identifying the product by National Stock Number (NSN) and the government contract number. Code 39 was recommended in 1981 by the Distribution Symbology Study Group (DSSG) for the labeling of corrugated shipping containers with alphanumeric information. The Automotive Industry Action Group (AIAG) bar code standard recommends Code 39 symbology, and Code 39 enjoys similar status in the health care industry's Health Industry Bar Code (HIBC) standard issued in 1984. In mid-1983, the French pharmaceutical industry adopted Code 39 as a national standard for pharmaceutical product marking. Code 39 is also one of the three symbologies identified in the American National Standards Institute (ANSI) standard MH 10.8M-1983. Code 39 is further recommended by the aluminum industry, the EMBARC standard, and standards promulgated by the International Air Transport Association (IATA).

The name Code 39 is both a descriptor of its original character set of 39 characters (currently, Code 39 has 43 characters) and the structure of the code, namely that three of the nine elements per character are wide, with the remaining six being narrow. Each character in Code 39 is represented by a group of five bars and four spaces. The complete character set includes a start/stop character (conventionally decoded as an asterisk) and 43 data characters consisting of the 10 digits, the 26 letters of the alphabet, space, and the six symbols -, ., $, /, +, and %.

The strong self-checking property of Code 39 provides a high level of data security. With properly designed scanning equipment and excellent quality symbol printing, you can expect only one substitution error out of 70 million characters scanned. Bar code printed by a well-maintained, better quality dot-matrix printer typically will provide less than one substitution error in 3 million characters scanned. The U.S. Department of Defense, in its LOGMARS testing, reported four substitution errors out of 563,243 bar code labels. These labels were separately reported to average 24 characters in length. Thus, in this practical test, 3,379,458 bar code characters were scanned for each substitution error. Bar code symbols in the LOGMARS test were printed by various means, including printing presses, formed font impact printers, and dot-matrix printers. For those applications that require exceptional data security, an optional check character is often used. The Health Industry Bar Code (HIBC) includes such a check character implementation, due to the high level of data integrity required in patient care.

Code 39 is one of two bar code symbologies (as of January 1, 1986) that have independently developed empirical test results regarding data security. The other symbology is Codabar. The testing done by the Distribution Symbology Study Group was to establish whether bar codes could be printed directly on corrugated shipping containers. Several symbologies were tested; Interleaved 2 of 5 and Code 39 were found acceptable.

Code 39 is a variable length code whose maximum length depends upon the reading equipment used. Code 39 is self-checking and does not require a check character in normal commercial and industrial applications. Code 39 characters are discrete with a range of intercharacter gaps permitted. Code 39 is bidirectional, meaning it can be scanned from left to right or right to left. The size of Code 39 is variable over a wide range, lending itself to light pen, hand-held laser, and fixed mounted scanner reading. High density Code 39 is 9.4 characters per inch, but densities as low as 1.4 characters per inch are included in the recommended practices of corrugated containers. A unique character, conventionally interpreted as an asterisk (*), is used exclusively for both a start

Figure 3-2. Code 39 character structure

---

and stop character. A Code 39 symbol consists of a leading quiet zone, a start character, appropriate data characters, a stop character, and a trailing quiet zone. In Code 39, wide elements are considered multiples of the narrow elements. The minimum nominal wide-to-narrow ratio is 2.0:1 and the maximum is 3.0:1.[1] The best first pass read rates and substitution error rates can be expected when the wide-to-narrow ratio is at its maximum of 3.0:1.

To achieve the standard density of 9.4 characters per inch, the nominal width of the narrow elements must be 7.5 mils and the wide-to-narrow ratio must be 2.25:1. When printed at a 3.0:1 ratio, the Code 39 character density with a 7.5-mil nominal narrow element width is 8.3 characters per inch. Figure 3-2 illustrates the character structure of a Code 39 character. Figure 3-3 shows the Code 39 character set, with its bar/space configurations. Figure 3-4 shows a sample HIBC Primary Symbol, encoded in Code 39. Table 3-2 lists various printing tolerances for the Code 39 symbology (see Appendix F, Code 39 Specifications, for more details).

CHAR.	PATTERN	BARS	SPACES	CHAR.	PATTERN	BARS	SPACES
1		10001	0100	M		11000	0001
2		01001	0100	N		00101	0001
3		11000	0100	O		10100	0001
4		00101	0100	P		01100	0001
5		10100	0100	Q		00011	0001
6		01100	0100	R		10010	0001
7		00011	0100	S		01010	0001
8		10010	0100	T		00110	0001
9		01010	0100	U		10001	1000
0		00110	0100	V		01001	1000
A		10001	0010	W		11000	1000
B		01001	0010	X		00101	1000
C		11000	0010	Y		10100	1000
D		00101	0010	Z		01100	1000
E		10100	0010	-		00011	1000
F		01100	0010	•		10010	1000
G		00011	0010	SPACE		01010	1000
H		10010	0010	*		00110	1000
I		01010	0010	$		00000	1110
J		00110	0010	/		00000	1101
K		10001	0001	+		00000	1011
L		01001	0001	%		00000	0111

The ∗ symbol denotes a unique start/stop character which must be the first and last character of every bar code symbol.

Figure 3-3. Code 39 character set

* +A123B4C5D6E711 *

Figure 3-4. HIBC Primary Symbol